Prayer Companion for Eucharistic Adoration

I0798831

Our Sunday Visitor
Huntington, Indiana

Cover image: *A Monstrance*, artist unknown, National Gallery of Art.

ISBN: 978-1-63966-168-8 (Inventory No. T2871)
First printing, January 2020
Digital edition, June 2021
Current printing, 2025, published by OSV, Our Sunday Visitor, 200 Noll Plaza, Huntington, IN 46750; www.osv.com; 1-800-348-2440

CONTENTS

Old Testament Scripture

Genesis 2-3 [*excerpts*]
Creation and Fall 1

Genesis 14:18-20
The Offering of Melchizedek 3

Exodus 12 [*excerpts*]
The Passover Ritual 3

Exodus 16 [*excerpts*]
Manna from Heaven 6

Exodus 24:3-8
The Covenant. .10

Deuteronomy 8:1-16
Covenant Blessings. 11

1 Kings 19:3-18
Elijah's Flight to Horeb. 13

Isaiah 53
Pierced for Our Sins. 16

Isaiah 55
An Invitation to Grace 19

Proverbs 9:1-6
Wisdom's Invitation. 22

Psalms

Psalm 23 (22)
The Lord Is My Shepherd 23

Psalm 24 (23)
The King of Glory 24

Psalm 34 (33)
Praise and Glorify God 25

Psalm 78 (77):1-29
Bread of Angels 28

Psalm 91 (90)
The Shelter of the Most High 32

Psalm 116B (114:10-19; 115)
The Cup of Salvation 34

Psalm 145 (144)
Proclaiming the Works of the Lord . . 35

The Gospels

Matthew 26:26-30
The Lord's Supper 38

Mark 6:30-33
Rest with Jesus 38

Luke 24:13-35
Road to Emmaus 39

John 6:1-15
Multiplication of the Loaves 41

John 6:22-35
Bread of Life 43

John 6:37-69
Living Bread from Heaven 45

John 19:28-37
"It Is Finished" 48

New Testament Scripture

Acts 2:42-47
The Apostles Break Bread 50

Acts 10:34-43
Eating and Drinking with the Lord . . 51

1 Corinthians 10:14-22
Participation in the Body of Christ . . 52

1 Corinthians 11:23-29
Eucharistic Remembrance 53

Hebrews 9:11-26
The New Covenant 54

Hebrews 12:14-24
Blood More Eloquent
Than That of Abel 56

1 Peter 1:17-21
A Spotless Unblemished Lamb 58

1 John 5:1-8
The Spirit, the Water, and the Blood Testify. 59

Revelation 1:4-8
Every Eye Will See Him 60

Revelation 12:10-11
The Blood of the Lamb 61

Prayers and Hymns

Anima Christi 63

Prayer of Self-Offering. 64

O Salutaris Hostia 64

Prayer to Our Lord Jesus Christ Crucified. 65

The Universal Prayer Attributed to Pope Clement XI . . . 66

Tantum Ergo 69

O Sacrum Convivium. 70

Divine Praises 70

Adoro Te Devote 71

Ave Verum Corpus 73

Corpus Christi Sequence
(*Lauda Sion*) 74

Ubi Caritas 78

Litanies

Litany of the
Holy Name of Jesus 79

Litany of the
Sacred Heart of Jesus 85

Litany of the
Most Precious Blood 90

Litany of the
Holy Eucharist 94

Excerpts from Papal Documents

Venerable Pius XII,
Mystici Corporis Christi
(*On the Mystical Body of Christ*) . . . 98

St. John XXIII,
Sacerdotii Nostri Primordia
(On St. John Vianney) 100

St. Paul VI, *Marialis Cultus*
(On Devotion to the
Bl. Virgin Mary) 102

St. Paul VI,
Mysterium Fidei
(On the Holy Eucharist) 105

St. John Paul II,
Ecclesia de Eucharistia
(On the Eucharist) 108

St. John Paul II,
Dominicae Cenae
(On the Mystery and
Worship of the Eucharist) 110

Pope Benedict XVI,
Sacramentum Caritatis
(The Sacrament of Charity) 116

Pope Benedict, *Meditation*
During the Eucharistic
Procession in Lourdes 118

Pope Francis, *Gaudete et Exsultate* (*Rejoice and Be Glad*) 119

Excerpt from a Bishops' Pastoral Statement

The Eucharist and the Hungers of the Human Family 120

OLD TESTAMENT SCRIPTURE

Genesis 2-3 [*excerpts*] *Creation and Fall*

(Gn 2:7-9; Gn 3:6-13, 22-24)

Then the LORD God formed the man out of the dust of the ground and blew into his nostrils the breath of life, and the man became a living being.

The LORD God planted a garden in Eden, in the east, and placed there the man whom he had formed. Out of the ground the LORD God made grow every tree that was delightful to look at and good for food, with the tree of life in the middle of the garden and the tree of the knowledge of good and evil. …

The woman saw that the tree was good for food and pleasing to the eyes, and the tree was desirable for gaining wisdom. So she took some of its fruit and ate it; and she also gave some to her husband, who was with her, and he ate it. Then the eyes of both of them were opened, and they knew that they were naked; so they sewed fig leaves together and made loincloths for themselves.

When they heard the sound of the LORD God walking about in the garden at the breezy time of the day, the man and his wife hid themselves from the LORD God among the trees of the garden. The LORD God then called to the man and asked him: Where are you? He answered, "I heard you in the garden; but I was afraid, because I was naked, so I hid." Then God asked: Who told you that you were naked? Have you eaten from the tree of which I had forbidden you to eat? The man replied, "The woman whom you put here with me—she gave me fruit from the tree, so I ate it." The LORD God then asked the woman: What is this you have done? The woman answered, "The snake tricked me, so I ate it."...

Then the LORD God said: See! The man has become like one of us, knowing good and evil! Now, what if he also reaches out his hand to take fruit from the tree of life, and eats of it and lives forever? The LORD God therefore banished him from the garden of Eden, to till the ground from which he had been taken. He expelled the man, stationing the cherubim and the fiery revolving sword east of the garden of Eden, to guard the way to the tree of life.

Genesis 14:18-20
The Offering of Melchizedek

Melchizedek, king of Salem, brought out bread and wine. He was a priest of God Most High. He blessed Abram with these words:

"Blessed be Abram by God Most High,
the creator of heaven and earth;
And blessed be God Most High,
who delivered your foes into your hand."

Then Abram gave him a tenth of everything.

Exodus 12 [*excerpts*]
The Passover Ritual

(Verses 1, 3, 5, 7-8, 11-14, 17, 21-28)

The LORD said to Moses and Aaron in the land of Egypt: … Tell the whole community of Israel: On the tenth of this month every family must procure for itself a lamb … Your lamb must be a year-old male and without blemish. You may take it from either the sheep or the goats. … They will take some of its blood and apply it to the two doorposts and the lintel of the houses in which they eat it. They will consume its meat that same night, eating it roasted with unleavened bread and bitter herbs. …

This is how you are to eat it: with your loins girt, sandals on your feet and your staff in hand, you will eat it in a hurry. It is the LORD's Passover. For on this same night I will go through Egypt, striking down every firstborn in the land, human being and beast alike, and executing judgment on all the gods of Egypt—I, the LORD! But for you the blood will mark the houses where you are. Seeing the blood, I will pass over you; thereby, when I strike the land of Egypt, no destructive blow will come upon you.

This day will be a day of remembrance for you, which your future generations will celebrate with pilgrimage to the LORD; you will celebrate it as a statute forever. ... Keep, then, the custom of the unleavened bread, since it was on this very day that I brought your armies out of the land of Egypt. You must observe this day throughout your generations as a statute forever.

Promulgation of the Passover.

Moses summoned all the elders of Israel and said to them, "Go and procure lambs for your families, and slaughter the Passover victims. Then take a bunch of hyssop, and dipping it in the blood that is in the basin, apply some of this blood to the lintel and the two doorposts. And none of you shall go outdoors until morning. For when the LORD goes by to strike down the Egyptians, seeing the blood on the lintel and the two doorposts, the LORD will pass over that door and not let the destroyer come into your houses to strike you down.

"You will keep this practice forever as a statute for yourselves and your descendants. Thus, when you have entered the land which the Lord will give you as he promised, you must observe this rite. When your children ask you, 'What does this rite of yours mean?' you will reply, 'It is the Passover sacrifice for the Lord, who passed over the houses of the Israelites in Egypt; when he struck down the Egyptians, he delivered our houses.'"

Then the people knelt and bowed down, and the Israelites went and did exactly as the Lord had commanded Moses and Aaron.

Exodus 16 [*excerpts*] *Manna from Heaven*

(Verses 1-15, 25-35)

The Wilderness of Sin.

Having set out from Elim, the whole

Israelite community came into the wilderness of Sin, which is between Elim and Sinai. … Here in the wilderness the whole Israelite community grumbled against Moses and Aaron. The Israelites said to them, "If only we had died at the LORD's hand in the land of Egypt, as we sat by our kettles of meat and ate our fill of bread! But you have led us into this wilderness to make this whole assembly die of famine!"

The Quail and the Manna.

Then the LORD said to Moses: I am going to rain down bread from heaven for you. Each day the people are to go out and gather their daily portion; thus will I test them, to see whether they follow my instructions or not. On the sixth day, however, when they prepare what they bring in, let it be twice as much as they gather on the other days. So Moses and Aaron told all the Israelites, "At evening you will know that it was the LORD who brought you out of the land of Egypt; and in the morning you will see the glory of the LORD, when he hears your grumbling against him.

But who are we that you should grumble against us?" And Moses said, "When the LORD gives you meat to eat in the evening and in the morning your fill of bread, and hears the grumbling you utter against him, who then are we? Your grumbling is not against us, but against the LORD."

Then Moses said to Aaron, "Tell the whole Israelite community: Approach the LORD, for he has heard your grumbling." But while Aaron was speaking to the whole Israelite community, they turned in the direction of the wilderness, and there the glory of the LORD appeared in the cloud! The LORD said to Moses: I have heard the grumbling of the Israelites. Tell them: In the evening twilight you will eat meat, and in the morning you will have your fill of bread, and then you will know that I, the LORD, am your God.

In the evening, quail came up and covered the camp. In the morning there was a layer of dew all about the camp, and when the layer of dew evaporated, fine flakes were on the surface of the wilderness, fine flakes like hoarfrost on the ground. On seeing it, the Israelites asked one another, "What is this?" for they did not know what it was. But Moses told them, "It is the bread which the LORD has given you to eat.

Regulations Regarding the Manna.

... Moses then said, "Eat it today, for today is the sabbath of the LORD. Today you will not find any in the field. Six days you will gather it, but on the seventh day, the sabbath, it will not be there." Still, on the seventh day some of the people went out to gather it, but they did not find any. Then the LORD said to Moses: How long will you refuse to keep my commandments and my instructions? Take note! The LORD has given you the sabbath. That is why on the sixth day he gives you food for two days. Each of you stay where you are and let no one go out on the seventh day. After that the people rested on the seventh day.

The house of Israel named this food manna. It was like coriander seed, white, and it tasted like wafers made with honey.

Moses said, "This is what the LORD has

commanded. Keep a full omer of it for your future generations, so that they may see the food I gave you to eat in the wilderness when I brought you out of the land of Egypt." Moses then told Aaron, "Take a jar and put a full omer of manna in it. Then place it before the LORD to keep it for your future generations." As the LORD had commanded Moses, Aaron placed it in front of the covenant to keep it.

The Israelites ate the manna for forty years, until they came to settled land; they ate the manna until they came to the borders of Canaan.

Exodus 24:3-8
The Covenant

When Moses came to the people and related all the words and ordinances of the LORD, they all answered with one voice, "We will do everything that the LORD has told us." Moses then wrote down all the words of the LORD and, rising early in the morning, he built at the foot of the mountain an altar and twelve sacred stones for the twelve tribes of Israel. Then, having sent young men of the Israelites to offer burnt offerings and sacrifice young bulls as communion offerings to the LORD, Moses took half of the blood and put it in large bowls; the other half he splashed on the altar. Taking the book of the covenant, he read it aloud to the people, who answered, "All that the LORD has said, we will hear and do." Then he took the blood and splashed it on the people, saying, "This is the blood of the covenant which the LORD has made with you according to all these words."

Deuteronomy 8:1-16
Covenant Blessings

God's Care

Be careful to observe this whole commandment that I enjoin on you today, that you may live and increase, and may enter in and possess the land which the LORD promised on oath to your ancestors. Remember how for these forty years the LORD, your God, has directed all your journeying in the wilderness, so as to test you by affliction, to know what was in your heart: to keep his commandments, or not. He therefore let you be afflicted with hunger, and then fed you with manna, a food unknown to you and your ancestors, so you might know that it is not by bread alone that people live, but by all that comes forth from the mouth of the LORD. The clothing did not fall from you in tatters, nor did your feet swell these forty years. So you must know in your heart that, even as a man disciplines his son, so the LORD, your God, disciplines you. Therefore, keep the commandments of the LORD, your God, by walking in his ways and fearing him.

Cautions About Prosperity

For the LORD, your God, is bringing you into a good country, a land with streams of water, with springs and fountains welling up in the hills and valleys, a land of wheat and barley, of vines and fig trees and pomegranates, of olive trees and of honey, a land where you will always have bread and where you will lack nothing, a land whose stones contain iron and in whose hills you can mine copper. But when you have eaten and are satisfied, you must bless the LORD, your God, for the good land he has given you. Be careful not to forget the LORD, your God, by failing to keep his commandments and ordinances and statutes which I enjoin on you today: lest, when you have eaten and are satisfied, and have built fine houses and lived in them, and your herds and flocks have increased, your silver and gold has increased, and all your property has increased, you then become haughty of heart and forget the LORD, your God, who brought you out of the land of Egypt, that house of slavery; he guided you through the vast and terrible wilderness with its saraph serpents and scorpions, its parched and waterless ground; he brought forth water for you from the flinty rock and fed you in the wilderness with manna, a food unknown to your ancestors, that he might afflict you and test you, but also make you prosperous in the end.

1 Kings 19:3-18
Elijah's Flight to Horeb

Elijah was afraid and fled for his life, going to Beer-sheba of Judah. He left his servant there and went a day's journey into the wilderness, until he came to a solitary broom tree and sat beneath it. He prayed for death: "Enough, LORD! Take my life, for I am no better than my ancestors." He lay down and fell asleep under the solitary broom tree, but suddenly a messenger touched him and said, "Get up and eat!" He looked and there at his head was a hearth cake and a jug of water. After he ate and drank, he lay down again, but the angel of the LORD came back a second time, touched him, and said, "Get up and eat or the journey will be too much for you!" He got up, ate, and drank; then strengthened by that food, he walked forty days and forty nights to the mountain of God, Horeb.

There he came to a cave, where he took shelter. But the word of the LORD came to him: Why are you here, Elijah? He answered: "I have been most zealous for the LORD, the God of hosts, but the Israelites have forsaken your covenant. They have destroyed your altars and murdered your prophets by the sword. I alone remain, and they seek to take my life." Then the LORD said: Go out and stand on the mountain before the LORD; the LORD will pass by. There was a strong and violent wind rending the mountains and crushing rocks before the LORD—but the LORD was not in the wind; after the wind, an earthquake—but the LORD was not in the earthquake; after the earthquake, fire—but the LORD was not in the fire; after the fire, a light silent sound.

When he heard this, Elijah hid his face in his cloak and went out and stood at the entrance of the cave. A voice said to him, Why are you here, Elijah? He replied, "I have been most zealous for the LORD, the God of hosts, but the Israelites have forsaken your covenant. They have destroyed your altars and murdered your prophets by the sword. I alone remain, and they seek to take my life." The LORD said to him: Go back! Take the desert road to Damascus. When you arrive, you shall anoint Hazael as king of

Aram. You shall also anoint Jehu, son of Nimshi, as king of Israel, and Elisha, son of Shaphat of Abel-meholah, as prophet to succeed you. Anyone who escapes the sword of Hazael, Jehu will kill. Anyone who escapes the sword of Jehu, Elisha will kill. But I will spare seven thousand in Israel—every knee that has not bent to Baal, every mouth that has not kissed him.

Isaiah 53
Pierced for Our Sins

Who would believe what we have heard?
To whom has the arm of the LORD
been revealed?

He grew up like a sapling before him,
like a shoot from the parched earth;
He had no majestic bearing to catch
our eye,
no beauty to draw us to him.
He was spurned and avoided by men,
a man of suffering, knowing pain,
Like one from whom you turn your face,
spurned, and we held him in no esteem.

Yet it was our pain that he bore,

our sufferings he endured.
We thought of him as stricken,
struck down by God and afflicted,
But he was pierced for our sins,
crushed for our iniquity.
He bore the punishment that makes
us whole,
by his wounds we were healed.
We had all gone astray like sheep,
all following our own way;
But the LORD laid upon him
the guilt of us all.

Though harshly treated, he submitted
and did not open his mouth;
Like a lamb led to slaughter
or a sheep silent before shearers,
he did not open his mouth.
Seized and condemned, he was taken
away.
Who would have thought any more of
his destiny?
For he was cut off from the land of
the living,
struck for the sins of his people.
He was given a grave among the wicked,
a burial place with evildoers,

Though he had done no wrong,
 nor was deceit found in his mouth.
But it was the LORD's will to crush him
 with pain.
By making his life as a reparation
 offering,
 he shall see his offspring, shall
 lengthen his days,
 and the LORD's will shall be accom-
 plished through him.
Because of his anguish he shall see the
 light;
 because of his knowledge he shall be
 content;
My servant, the just one, shall justify the
 many,
 their iniquity he shall bear.
Therefore I will give him his portion
 among the many,
 and he shall divide the spoils with the
 mighty,
Because he surrendered himself to
 death,
 was counted among the transgressors,
Bore the sins of many,
 and interceded for the transgressors.

Isaiah 55
An Invitation to Grace

All you who are thirsty,
  come to the water!
You who have no money,
  come, buy grain and eat;
Come, buy grain without money,
  wine and milk without cost!
Why spend your money for what is not
    bread;
  your wages for what does not satisfy?
Only listen to me, and you shall eat
    well,
  you shall delight in rich fare.
Pay attention and come to me;
  listen, that you may have life.
I will make with you an everlasting
    covenant,
  the steadfast loyalty promised to
    David.
As I made him a witness to peoples,
  a leader and commander of peoples,
So shall you summon a nation you
    knew not,
  and a nation that knew you not shall

run to you,
Because of the Lord, your God,
the Holy One of Israel, who has
glorified you.

Seek the Lord while he may be found,
call upon him while he is near.
Let the wicked forsake their way,
and sinners their thoughts;
Let them turn to the Lord to find mercy;
to our God, who is generous in
forgiving.
For my thoughts are not your thoughts,
nor are your ways my ways—oracle of
the Lord.
For as the heavens are higher than
the earth,
so are my ways higher than your ways,
my thoughts higher than your thoughts.

Yet just as from the heavens
the rain and snow come down
And do not return there
till they have watered the earth,
making it fertile and fruitful,

Giving seed to the one who sows
  and bread to the one who eats,
So shall my word be
  that goes forth from my mouth;
It shall not return to me empty,
  but shall do what pleases me,
  achieving the end for which I sent it.

Yes, in joy you shall go forth,
  in peace you shall be brought home;
Mountains and hills shall break out in
    song before you,
  all trees of the field shall clap their
    hands.
In place of the thornbush, the cypress
    shall grow,
  instead of nettles, the myrtle.
This shall be to the LORD's renown,
  as an everlasting sign that shall
    not fail.

Proverbs 9:1-6
Wisdom's Invitation

Wisdom has built her house,
  she has set up her seven columns;
She has prepared her meat, mixed
    her wine,
  yes, she has spread her table.
She has sent out her maidservants;
    she calls
  from the heights out over the city:
"Let whoever is naive turn in here;
  to any who lack sense I say,
Come, eat of my food,
  and drink of the wine I have mixed!
Forsake foolishness that you may live;
  advance in the way of understanding."

PSALMS

Psalm 23 (22)
The Lord Is My Shepherd

1 *A Psalm of David.*

The LORD is my shepherd;
there is nothing I shall want.
2 Fresh and green are the pastures
where he gives me repose.
Near restful waters he leads me;
3 he revives my soul.

He guides me along the right path,
for the sake of his name.
4 Though I should walk in the valley of
the shadow of death,
no evil would I fear, for you are with me.
Your crook and your staff will give
me comfort.

5 You have prepared a table before me
in the sight of my foes.
My head you have anointed with oil;
my cup is overflowing.

6 Surely goodness and mercy shall
follow me
all the days of my life.
In the LORD's own house shall I dwell
for length of days unending.

Psalm 24 (23)
The King of Glory

1 *A Psalm of David.*

The LORD's is the earth and its fullness,
the world, and those who dwell in it.
2 It is he who set it on the seas;
on the rivers he made it firm.

3 Who shall climb the mountain of
the LORD?
Who shall stand in his holy place?
4 The clean of hands and pure of heart,
whose soul is not set on vain things,
who has not sworn deceitful words.

5 Blessings from the LORD shall he receive,
and right reward from the God who
saves him.
6 Such are the people who seek him,
who seek the face of the God of Jacob.

* * *

7 O gates, lift high your heads;
grow higher, ancient doors.
Let him enter, the king of glory!

8 Who is this king of glory?
The LORD, the mighty, the valiant;
the LORD, the valiant in war.

9 O gates, lift high your heads;
grow higher, ancient doors.
Let him enter, the king of glory!

10 Who is this king of glory?
He, the LORD of hosts,
he is the king of glory.

Psalm 34 (33)
Praise and Glorify God

1 *Of David, when he feigned madness before Abimelech, so that he drove him out, and he went away.*

2 I will bless the LORD at all times,
praise of him is always in my mouth.
3 In the LORD my soul shall make
its boast;
the humble shall hear and be glad.

4 Glorify the LORD with me;
together let us praise his name.
5 I sought the LORD, and he
answered me;
from all my terrors he set me free.

6 Look toward him and be radiant;
let your faces not be abashed.
7 This lowly one called; the LORD heard,
and rescued him from all his distress.

8 The angel of the LORD is encamped
around those who fear him, to
rescue them.
9 Taste and see that the LORD is good.
Blessed the man who seeks refuge in
him.

10 Fear the LORD, you his holy ones.
They lack nothing, those who fear him.
11 The rich suffer want and go hungry,
but those who seek the LORD lack
no blessing.

12 Come, children, and hear me,
that I may teach you the fear of
the LORD.
13 Who is it that desires life
and longs to see prosperous days?

[14] Guard your tongue from evil,
and your lips from speaking deceit.
[15] Turn aside from evil and do good.
Seek after peace, and pursue it.

[16] The LORD turns his eyes to the just one,
and his ears are open to his cry.
[17] The LORD turns his face against
the wicked
to cut off their remembrance from
the earth.

[18] When the just one cries out, the
LORD hears,
and rescues him in all his distress.
[19] The LORD is close to the
brokenhearted;
those whose spirit is crushed he
will save.

[20] Many are the trials of the just one,
but from them all the LORD will
rescue him.
[21] He will keep guard over all his bones;
not one of his bones shall be broken.

22 Evil brings death to the wicked;
those who hate the just one
are doomed.
23 The LORD ransoms the souls of his
servants.
All who trust in him shall not
be condemned.

Psalm 78 (77):1-29
Bread of Angels

1 *A Maskil of Asaph.*

Give ear, my people, to my teaching;
incline your ear to the words of
my mouth.
2 I will open my mouth in a parable
and utter hidden lessons of the past.

3 The things we have heard and
understood,
the things our fathers have told us,
4 these we will not hide from their
children
but will tell them to the next generation:
the glories of the LORD and his might,
and the marvelous deeds he has done.

5 He established a decree in Jacob;
in Israel he set up a law.
To our fathers he gave a command
to make it known to their children,
6 that the next generation might know it,
the children yet to be born.

They should arise and declare it to
their children,
7 that they should set their hope in God,
and never forget God's deeds,
but keep every one of his commands,

8 so that they might not be like their fathers,
a defiant and rebellious generation,
a generation whose heart was fickle,
whose spirit was not faithful to God.

9 The sons of Ephraim, armed with
the bow,
turned back on the day of battle.
10 They failed to keep God's covenant,
refused to walk according to his law.

11 They forgot the things he had done,
the wondrous works he had shown them.
12 He did wonders in the sight of
their fathers,
in Egypt, in the plains of Zoan.

13 He divided the sea and led them
through,
and made the waters stand up like a wall.
14 By day he led them with a cloud;
throughout the night, with a light of fire.

15 He split the rocks in the desert.
He gave them plentiful drink, as from
the deep.
16 He made streams flow out from
the rock,
and made waters run down like rivers.

17 Yet still they sinned against him,
rebelled against the Most High in
the desert.
18 In their heart they put God to the test
by demanding the food they craved.

19 They spoke against God and said:
"Can God spread a table in the
wilderness?
20 See, he struck the rock:
water gushed forth and swept down
in torrents.
But can he also give us bread?
Can he provide meat for his people?"

21 When he heard this, the LORD
was angry.
A fire was kindled against Jacob;
his anger rose against Israel.
22 For they had no faith in God,
and did not trust his saving power.

23 Yet he commanded the clouds above,
and opened the gates of heaven.
24 He rained down manna to eat,
and gave them bread from heaven.

25 Man ate the bread of angels.
He sent them abundance of food;
26 the east wind he stirred up in
the heavens,
the south wind he directed by his might.

27 He rained flesh upon them like dust,
winged fowl like the sands of the sea.
28 He let it fall in the midst of their
camp,
and all around their tents.
29 So they ate and had their fill,
what they craved, he gave them.

Psalm 91 (90)
The Shelter of the Most High

1 He who dwells in the shelter of the
Most High,
and abides in the shade of the Almighty,
2 says to the Lord, "My refuge,
my stronghold, my God in whom I
trust!"

3 He will free you from the snare of
the fowler,
from the destructive plague;
4 he will conceal you with his pinions,
and under his wings you will
find refuge.
His faithfulness is buckler and shield.

5 You will not fear the terror of the night,
nor the arrow that flies by day,
6 nor the plague that prowls in
the darkness,
nor the scourge that lays waste at noon.

7 A thousand may fall at your side,
ten thousand fall at your right:
you it will never approach.

8 Your eyes have only to look
to see how the wicked are repaid.
9 For you, O Lord, are my refuge.
You have made the Most High
your dwelling.

10 Upon you no evil shall fall,
no plague approach your tent.
11 For you has he commanded his angels
to keep you in all your ways.

12 They shall bear you upon their hands,
lest you strike your foot against a stone.
13 On the lion and the viper you will
tread,
and trample the young lion and
the serpent.

14 Since he clings to me in love, I will
free him,
protect him, for he knows my name.
15 When he calls on me, I will
answer him;
I will be with him in distress;
I will deliver him, and give him glory.

16 With length of days I will content
him;

I will show him my saving power.

Psalm 116B (114:10-19; 115)
The Cup of Salvation

10 I trusted, even when I said,
"I am sorely afflicted,"
11 and when I said in my alarm,
"These people are all liars."

12 How can I repay the LORD
for all his goodness to me?
13 The cup of salvation I will raise;
I will call on the name of the LORD.

14 My vows to the LORD I will fulfill
before all his people.
15 How precious in the eyes of the LORD
is the death of his faithful.

16 Your servant, LORD, your servant am I,
the son of your handmaid;
you have loosened my bonds.
17 I will offer you a thanksgiving sacrifice;
I will call on the name of the LORD.

18 My vows to the LORD I will fulfill
before all his people,
19 in the courts of the house of the LORD,

in your midst, O Jerusalem.

Alleluia!

Psalm 145 (144)
Proclaiming the Works of the Lord

1 *Praise. Of David.*

I will extol you, my God and king,
and bless your name forever and ever.

2 I will bless you day after day,
and praise your name forever and ever.
3 The LORD is great and highly to
be praised;
his greatness cannot be measured.

4 Age to age shall proclaim your works,
shall declare your mighty deeds.
5 They will tell of your great glory
and splendor,
and recount your wonderful works.

6 They will speak of your awesome
deeds,
recount your greatness and might.
7 They will recall your abundant

goodness,
and sing of your righteous deeds
with joy.

8 The LORD is kind and full of compassion,
slow to anger, abounding in mercy.
9 How good is the LORD to all,
compassionate to all his creatures.

10 All your works shall thank you, O LORD,
and all your faithful ones bless you.
11 They shall speak of the glory of
your reign,
and declare your mighty deeds,

12 to make known your might to the
whole human race,
and the glorious splendor of your reign.
13 Your kingdom is an everlasting
kingdom;
your rule endures for all generations.

The LORD is faithful in all his words,
and holy in all his deeds.
14 The LORD supports all who fall,
and raises up all who are bowed down.

15 The eyes of all look to you,
and you give them their food in due

season.
16 You open your hand and satisfy
the desire of every living thing.

17 The LORD is just in all his ways,
and holy in all his deeds.
18 The LORD is close to all who call him,
who call on him in truth.

19 He fulfills the desires of those who
fear him;
he hears their cry and he saves them.
20 The LORD keeps watch over all who
love him;
the wicked he will utterly destroy.

21 Let my mouth speak the praise of the
LORD;
let all flesh bless his holy name
forever, for ages unending.

THE GOSPELS

Matthew 26:26-30
The Lord's Supper

While they were eating, Jesus took bread, said the blessing, broke it, and giving it to his disciples said, "Take and eat; this is my body." Then he took a cup, gave thanks, and gave it to them, saying, "Drink from it, all of you, for this is my blood of the covenant, which will be shed on behalf of many for the forgiveness of sins. I tell you, from now on I shall not drink this fruit of the vine until the day when I drink it with you new in the kingdom of my Father." Then, after singing a hymn, they went out to the Mount of Olives.

Mark 6:30-33
Rest with Jesus

The apostles gathered together with Jesus and reported all they had done and taught. He said to them, "Come away by yourselves to a deserted place and rest a while." People were coming and going in great numbers, and they had no opportunity even to eat. So they went off in the boat by themselves to a deserted place. People saw them leaving and many came to know about it. They hastened there on foot from all the towns and arrived at the place before them.

Luke 24:13-35
Road to Emmaus

Now that very day two of them were going to a village seven miles from Jerusalem called Emmaus, and they were conversing about all the things that had occurred. And it happened that while they were conversing and debating, Jesus himself drew near and walked with them, but their eyes were prevented from recognizing him. He asked them, "What are you discussing as you walk along?" They stopped, looking downcast. One of them, named Cleopas, said to him in reply, "Are you the only visitor to Jerusalem who does not know of the things that have taken place there in these days?" And he replied to them, "What sort of things?" They said to him, "The things that happened to Jesus the Nazarene, who was a prophet mighty in deed and word before God and all the people, how our chief priests and rulers both handed him over to a sentence of death and crucified him. But we were hoping that he would be the one to redeem Israel; and besides all this, it is now the third day since this took place. Some women from our group, however, have astounded us: they were at the tomb early in the morning and did not find his body; they came back and reported that they had indeed seen a vision of angels who announced that he was alive. Then some of those with us went to the tomb and found things just as the women had described, but him they did not see." And he said to them, "Oh, how foolish you are! How slow of heart to believe all that the prophets spoke! Was it not necessary that the Messiah should suffer these things and enter into his glory?" Then beginning with Moses and all the prophets, he interpreted to them what referred to him in all the scriptures. As they approached the village to which they were going, he gave the impression that he was going on farther. But they urged him, "Stay with us, for it is nearly evening and the day is almost over." So he went in to stay with them. And it happened that, while he was with them at table, he took bread, said the blessing, broke it, and gave it to them. With that their eyes were opened and they recognized him, but he vanished from their sight. Then they said to each other, "Were not our hearts burning [within us] while he spoke to us on the way and opened the scriptures to us?" So they set out at once and returned to Jerusalem where they found gathered together the eleven and those with them who were saying, "The Lord has truly been raised and has appeared to Simon!" Then the two recounted what had taken place on the way and how he was made known to them in the breaking of the bread.

John 6:1-15
Multiplication of the Loaves

After this, Jesus went across the Sea of Galilee [of Tiberias]. A large crowd followed him, because they saw the signs he was performing on the sick. Jesus went up on the mountain, and there he sat down with his disciples. The Jewish feast of Passover was near. When Jesus raised his eyes and saw that a large crowd was coming to him, he said to Philip, "Where can we buy enough food for them to eat?" He said this to test him, because he himself knew what he was going to do. Philip answered him, "Two hundred days' wages worth of food would not be enough for each of them to have a little [bit]." One of his disciples, Andrew, the brother of Simon Peter, said to him, "There is a boy here who has five barley loaves and two fish; but what good are these for so many?" Jesus said, "Have the people recline." Now there was a great deal of grass in that place. So the men reclined, about five thousand in number. Then Jesus took the loaves, gave thanks, and distributed them to those who were reclining, and also as much of the fish as they wanted. When they had had their fill, he said to his disciples, "Gather the fragments left over, so that nothing will be wasted." So they collected them, and filled twelve wicker baskets with fragments from the five barley loaves that had been more than they could eat. When the people saw the sign he had done, they said, "This is truly the Prophet, the one who is to come into the world." Since Jesus knew that they were going to come and carry him off to make him king, he withdrew again to the mountain alone.

John 6:22-35
Bread of Life

The next day, the crowd that remained across the sea saw that there had been only one boat there, and that Jesus had not gone along with his disciples in the boat, but only his disciples had left. Other boats came from Tiberias near the place where they had eaten the bread when the Lord gave thanks. When the crowd saw that neither Jesus nor his disciples were there, they themselves got into boats and came to Capernaum looking for Jesus. And when they found him across the sea they said to him, "Rabbi, when did you get here?" Jesus answered them and said,

"Amen, amen, I say to you, you are looking for me not because you saw signs but because you ate the loaves and were filled. Do not work for food that perishes but for the food that endures for eternal life, which the Son of Man will give you. For on him the Father, God, has set his seal." So they said to him, "What can we do to accomplish the works of God?" Jesus answered and said to them, "This is the work of God, that you believe in the one he sent." So they said to him, "What sign can you do, that we may see and believe in you? What can you do? Our ancestors ate manna in the desert, as it is written:

> 'He gave them bread from heaven
> to eat.'"

So Jesus said to them, "Amen, amen, I say to you, it was not Moses who gave the bread from heaven; my Father gives you the true bread from heaven. For the bread of God is that which comes down from heaven and gives life to the world."

So they said to him, "Sir, give us this bread always." Jesus said to them, "I am the bread of life; whoever comes to me will never hunger, and whoever believes in me will never thirst.

John 6:37-69
Living Bread from Heaven

"Everything that the Father gives me will come to me, and I will not reject anyone who comes to me, because I came down from heaven not to do my own will but the will of the one who sent me. And this is the will of the one who sent me, that I should not lose anything of what he gave me, but that I should raise it [on] the last day. For this is the will of my Father, that everyone who sees the Son and believes in him may have eternal life, and I shall raise him [on] the last day."

The Jews murmured about him because he said, "I am the bread that came down from heaven," and they said, "Is this not Jesus, the son of Joseph? Do we not know his father and mother? Then how can he say, 'I have come down from heaven'?" Jesus answered and said to them, "Stop murmuring among yourselves. No one can come to me unless the Father who sent me draw him, and I will raise him on the last day. It is written in the prophets:

'They shall all be taught by God.'

Everyone who listens to my Father and learns from him comes to me. Not that anyone has seen the Father except the one who is from God; he has seen the Father. Amen, amen, I say to you, whoever believes has eternal life. I am the bread of life. Your ancestors ate the manna in the desert, but they died; this is the bread that comes down from heaven so that one may eat it and not die. I am the living bread that came down from heaven; whoever eats this bread will live forever; and the bread that I will give is my flesh for the life of the world."

The Jews quarreled among themselves, saying, "How can this man give us [his] flesh to eat?" Jesus said to them, "Amen, amen, I say to you, unless you eat the flesh of the Son of Man and drink his blood, you do not have life within you. Whoever eats my flesh and drinks my blood has eternal life, and I will raise him on the last day. For my flesh is true food, and my blood is true drink. Whoever eats my flesh and drinks my blood remains in me and I in him. Just as the living Father sent me and I have life because of the Father, so also the one who feeds on me will have life because of me. This is the bread that came down from heaven. Unlike your ancestors who ate and still died, whoever eats this bread will live forever." These things he said while teaching in the synagogue in Capernaum.

The Words of Eternal Life.

Then many of his disciples who were listening said, "This saying is hard; who can accept it?" Since Jesus knew that his disciples were murmuring about this, he said to them, "Does this shock you? What if you were to see the Son of Man ascending to where he was before? It is the spirit that gives life, while the flesh is of no avail. The words I have spoken to you are spirit and life. But there are some of you who do not believe." Jesus knew from the beginning the ones who would not believe and the one who would betray him. And he said, "For this reason I have told you that no one can come to me unless it is granted him by my Father."

As a result of this, many [of] his disciples returned to their former way of life and no longer accompanied him. Jesus then said to the Twelve, "Do you also want to leave?" Simon Peter answered him, "Master, to whom shall we go? You have the words of eternal life. We have come to believe and are convinced that you are the Holy One of God."

John 19:28-37
"It Is Finished"

Aware that everything was now finished, in order that the scripture might be fulfilled, Jesus said, "I thirst." There was a vessel filled with common wine. So they put a sponge soaked in wine on a sprig of hyssop and put it up to his mouth. When Jesus had taken the wine, he said, "It is finished." And bowing his head, he handed over the spirit.

The Blood and Water.

Now since it was preparation day, in order that the bodies might not remain on the cross on the sabbath, for the sabbath day of that week was a solemn one, the Jews asked Pilate that their legs be broken and they be taken down. So the soldiers came and broke the legs of the first and then of the other one who was crucified with Jesus. But when they came to Jesus and saw that he was already dead, they did not break his legs, but one soldier thrust his lance into his side, and immediately blood and water flowed out. An eyewitness has testified, and his testimony is true; he knows that he is speaking the truth, so that you also may [come to] believe. For this happened so that the scripture passage might be fulfilled:

> "Not a bone of it will be broken."

And again another passage says:

> "They will look upon him whom
> they have pierced."

NEW TESTAMENT SCRIPTURE

Acts 2:42-47
The Apostles Break Bread

Communal Life.

They devoted themselves to the teaching of the apostles and to the communal life, to the breaking of the bread and to the prayers. Awe came upon everyone, and many wonders and signs were done through the apostles. All who believed were together and had all things in common; they would sell their property and possessions and divide them among all according to each one's need. Every day they devoted themselves to meeting together in the temple area and to breaking bread in their homes. They ate their meals with exultation and sincerity of heart, praising God and enjoying favor with all the people. And every day the Lord added to their number those who were being saved.

Acts 10:34-43
Eating and Drinking with the Lord

Peter's Speech.

Then Peter proceeded to speak and said, "In truth, I see that God shows no partiality. Rather, in every nation whoever fears him and acts uprightly is acceptable to him. You know the word [that] he sent to the Israelites as he proclaimed peace through Jesus Christ, who is Lord of all, what has happened all over Judea, beginning in Galilee after the baptism that John preached, how God anointed Jesus of Nazareth with the holy Spirit and power. He went about doing good and healing all those oppressed by the devil, for God was with him. We are witnesses of all that he did both in the country of the Jews and [in] Jerusalem. They put him to death by hanging him on a tree. This man God raised [on] the third day and granted that he be visible, not to all the people, but to us, the witnesses chosen by God in advance, who ate and drank with him after he rose from the dead. He commissioned us to preach to the people and testify that he is the one appointed by God as judge of the living and the dead. To him all the prophets bear witness, that everyone who believes in him will receive forgiveness of sins through his name."

1 Corinthians 10:14-22
Participation in the Body of Christ

Warning against Idolatry.

Therefore, my beloved, avoid idolatry. I am speaking as to sensible people; judge for yourselves what I am saying. The cup of blessing that we bless, is it not a participation in the blood of Christ? The bread that we break, is it not a participation in the body of Christ? Because the loaf of bread is one, we, though many, are one body, for we all partake of the one loaf.

Look at Israel according to the flesh; are not those who eat the sacrifices participants in the altar? So what am I saying?

That meat sacrificed to idols is anything? Or that an idol is anything? No, I mean that what they sacrifice, [they sacrifice] to demons, not to God, and I do not want you to become participants with demons. You cannot drink the cup of the Lord and also the cup of demons. You cannot partake of the table of the Lord and of the table of demons. Or are we provoking the Lord to jealous anger? Are we stronger than he?

1 Corinthians 11:23-29
Eucharistic Remembrance

For I received from the Lord what I also handed on to you, that the Lord Jesus, on the night he was handed over, took bread, and, after he had given thanks, broke it and said, "This is my body that is for you. Do this in remembrance of me." In the same way also the cup, after supper, saying, "This cup is the new covenant in my blood. Do this, as often as you drink it, in remembrance of me." For as often as you eat this bread and drink the cup, you proclaim the death of the Lord until he comes.

Therefore whoever eats the bread or drinks

the cup of the Lord unworthily will have to answer for the body and blood of the Lord. A person should examine himself, and so eat the bread and drink the cup. For anyone who eats and drinks without discerning the body, eats and drinks judgment on himself.

Hebrews 9:11-26
The New Covenant

Sacrifice of Jesus.

But when Christ came as high priest of the good things that have come to be, passing through the greater and more perfect tabernacle not made by hands, that is, not belonging to this creation, he entered once for all into the sanctuary, not with the blood of goats and calves but with his own blood, thus obtaining eternal redemption. For if the blood of goats and bulls and the sprinkling of a heifer's ashes can sanctify those who are defiled so that their flesh is cleansed, how much more will the blood of Christ, who through the eternal spirit offered himself unblemished to God, cleanse our consciences from dead works to worship the living God.

For this reason he is mediator of a new covenant: since a death has taken place for deliverance from transgressions under the first covenant, those who are called may receive the promised eternal inheritance. Now where there is a will, the death of the testator must be established. For a will takes effect only at death; it has no force while the testator is alive. Thus not even the first covenant was inaugurated without blood. When every commandment had been proclaimed by Moses to all the people according to the law, he took the blood of calves [and goats], together with water and crimson wool and hyssop, and sprinkled both the book itself and all the people, saying, "This is 'the blood of the covenant which God has enjoined upon you.'" In the same way, he sprinkled also the tabernacle and all the vessels of worship with blood. According to the law almost everything is purified by blood, and without the shedding of blood there is no forgiveness.

Therefore, it was necessary for the copies of the heavenly things to be purified by these rites, but the heavenly things themselves by better sacrifices than these.

For Christ did not enter into a sanctuary made by hands, a copy of the true one, but heaven itself, that he might now appear before God on our behalf. Not that he might offer himself repeatedly, as the high priest enters each year into the sanctuary with blood that is not his own; if that were so, he would have had to suffer repeatedly from the foundation of the world. But now once for all he has appeared at the end of the ages to take away sin by his sacrifice. Just as it is appointed that human beings die once, and after this the judgment, so also Christ, offered once to take away the sins of many, will appear a second time, not to take away sin but to bring salvation to those who eagerly await him.

Hebrews 12:14-29
Blood More Eloquent Than That of Abel

Penalties of Disobedience.

Strive for peace with everyone, and for that holiness without which no one will see the Lord. See to it that no one be deprived of the grace of God, that no bitter root spring up and cause trouble, through which many may become defiled, that no one be an immoral or profane person like Esau, who sold his birthright for a single meal. For you know that later, when he wanted to inherit his father's blessing, he was rejected because he found no opportunity to change his mind, even though he sought the blessing with tears.

You have not approached that which could be touched and a blazing fire and gloomy darkness and storm and a trumpet blast and a voice speaking words such that those who heard begged that no message be further addressed to them, for they could not bear to hear the command: "If even an animal touches the mountain, it shall be stoned." Indeed, so fearful was the spectacle that Moses said, "I am terrified and trembling." No, you have approached Mount Zion and the city of the living God, the heavenly Jerusalem, and countless angels in festal gathering, and the assembly of the firstborn enrolled in heaven, and God the judge of all, and the spirits of the just made perfect, and

Jesus, the mediator of a new covenant, and the sprinkled blood that speaks more eloquently than that of Abel.

See that you do not reject the one who speaks. For if they did not escape when they refused the one who warned them on earth, how much more in our case if we turn away from the one who warns from heaven. His voice shook the earth at that time, but now he has promised, "I will once more shake not only earth but heaven." That phrase, "once more," points to [the] removal of shaken, created things, so that what is unshaken may remain. Therefore, we who are receiving the unshakable kingdom should have gratitude, with which we should offer worship pleasing to God in reverence and awe. For our God is a consuming fire.

1 Peter 1:17-21
A Spotless Unblemished Lamb

Reverence.

Now if you invoke as Father him who judges impartially according to each one's works, conduct yourselves with reverence during the time of your sojourning, realizing that you were ransomed from your futile conduct, handed on by your ancestors, not with perishable things like silver or gold but with the precious blood of Christ as of a spotless unblemished lamb. He was known before the foundation of the world but revealed in the final time for you, who through him believe in God who raised him from the dead and gave him glory, so that your faith and hope are in God.

1 John 5:1-8
The Spirit, the Water, and the Blood Testify

Faith Is Victory over the World.

Everyone who believes that Jesus is the Christ is begotten by God, and everyone who loves the father loves [also] the one begotten by him. In this way we know that we love the children of God when we love God and obey his commandments. For the love of God is this, that we keep his commandments. And his commandments are not burdensome, for whoever is begotten by God conquers the world. And the victory that conquers the world is our faith. Who [indeed] is the victor over the world but the one who believes that Jesus is the Son of God?

This is the one who came through water and blood, Jesus Christ, not by water alone, but by water and blood. The Spirit is the one that testifies, and the Spirit is truth. So there are three that testify, the Spirit, the water, and the blood, and the three are of one accord.

Revelation 1:4-8
Every Eye Will See Him

Greeting.

John, to the seven churches in Asia: grace to you and peace from him who is and who was and who is to come, and from the seven spirits before his throne, and from Jesus Christ, the faithful witness, the firstborn of the dead and ruler of the kings of the earth. To him who loves us and has freed us from our sins by his blood, who has made us into a kingdom, priests for his God and Father, to him be glory and power forever [and ever]. Amen.

Behold, he is coming amid the
    clouds,
  and every eye will see him,
  even those who pierced him.
All the peoples of the earth will
    lament him.
  Yes. Amen.

"I am the Alpha and the Omega," says the Lord God, "the one who is and who was and who is to come, the almighty."

Revelation 12:10-11
The Blood of the Lamb

Then I heard a loud voice in heaven say:

"Now have salvation and power come,
  and the kingdom of our God
  and the authority of his Anointed.
For the accuser of our brothers is
    cast out,
  who accuses them before our God day
    and night.

They conquered him by the blood of the
Lamb
and by the word of their testimony;
love for life did not deter them from
death.

PRAYERS AND HYMNS

Anima Christi

(*Prayer to the Most Holy Redeemer*)

Soul of Christ, sanctify me.
Body of Christ, save me.
Blood of Christ, embolden me.
Water from the side of Christ, wash me.
Passion of Christ, strengthen me.
O good Jesus, hear me.
Within your wounds hide me.
Never permit me to be parted from you.
From the evil Enemy defend me.
At the hour of my death call me
and bid me come to you,
that with your Saints I may praise you
for age upon age.
Amen.

[from the *Roman Missal*]

Prayer of Self-Offering

Receive, Lord, my entire freedom.
Accept the whole of my memory,
my intellect and my will.
Whatever I have or possess,
it was you who gave it to me;
I restore it to you in full,
and I surrender it completely
to the guidance of your will.
Give me only love of you
together with your grace,
and I am rich enough
and ask for nothing more.
Amen.

[from the *Roman Missal*]

O Salutaris Hostia

O Victim bringing saving grace,
who open wide the gate of heav'n:
our foes assail and press us hard;
give us your strength, bring us your aid.

To you be everlasting praise
and glory, One and Triune Lord,
who grant us life that knows end,
for ever in our heav'nly home. Amen.

Prayer to Our Lord Jesus Christ Crucified

Behold, O good and loving Jesus,
that I cast myself on my knees before you
and, with the greatest fervor of spirit,
I pray and beseech you to instill into
my heart
ardent sentiments of faith, hope
and charity,
with true repentance for my sins
and a most firm purpose of amendment.
With deep affection and sorrow
I ponder intimately
and contemplate in my mind your
five wounds,
having before my eyes what the prophet
David
had already put in your mouth about
yourself, O good Jesus:
They have pierced my hands and my feet;
they have numbered all my bones (*Ps
21:17-18*).

[from the *Roman Missal*]

The Universal Prayer Attributed to Pope Clement XI

I believe, O Lord, but may I believe more firmly;
I hope, but may I hope more securely;
I love, but may I love more ardently;
I sorrow, but may I sorrow more deeply.

I adore you as my first beginning;
I long for you as my last end;
I praise you as my constant benefactor;
I invoke you as my gracious protector.

By your wisdom direct me,
by your righteousness restrain me,
by your indulgence console me,
by your power protect me.

I offer you, Lord, my thoughts to be directed to you,
my words, to be about you,
my deeds, to respect your will,
my trials, to be endured for you.

I will whatever you will,
I will it because you will it,
I will it in the way you will it,
I will it for as long as you will it.

Lord, enlighten my understanding, I pray:
arouse my will,
cleanse my heart,
sanctify my soul.

May I weep for past sins,
repel future temptations,
correct evil inclinations,
nurture appropriate virtues.

Give me, good God,
love for you, hatred for myself,
zeal for my neighbor,
contempt for the world.

May I strive to obey superiors,
to help those dependent on me,
to have care for my friends,
forgiveness for my enemies.

May I conquer sensuality by austerity,
avarice by generosity,
anger by gentleness,
lukewarmness by fervor.

Render me prudent in planning,
steadfast in dangers,
patient in adversity,
humble in prosperity.

Make me, O Lord, attentive at prayer,
moderate at meals,
diligent in work,
steadfast in intent.

May I be careful to maintain interior
innocence,
outward modesty,
exemplary behavior,
a regular life.

May I be always watchful in subduing nature,
in nourishing grace,
in observing your law,
in winning salvation.

May I learn from you
how precarious are earthly things,
how great divine things,
how fleeting is time,
how lasting things eternal.

Grant that I may prepare for death,
fear judgment,
flee hell,
gain paradise.
Through Christ our Lord.
Amen.

[from the *Roman Missal*]

Tantum Ergo

Let us, therefore, bow and worship
such a wondrous Sacrament;
let the ancient law and custom
to a newer rite now yield;
let our faith supply conviction
where the senses tire and fail.

To the Father, unbegotten,
and the Sole-begotten Son,
be salvation, blessing, honor,
jubilation, power, and praise;
to the One from both proceeding
equal glory and renown. Amen.

V. You have given them bread from heaven,

R. Having all delight within it.

Let us pray. O God, who in this wonderful Sacrament have left us a memorial of your Passion, grant us, we pray, so to revere the sacred mysteries of your Body and Blood that we may always experience in ourselves the fruits of your redemption. Who live and reign for ever and ever. Amen.

O Sacrum Convivium

O sacred banquet, in which Christ is received:
the memory of his Passion is renewed,
the mind is filled with grace,
and a pledge of future glory is given to us.

[from *Holy Communion and Worship of the Eucharist Outside Mass* (2024)]

Divine Praises

Blessed be God.
Blessed be his holy Name.
Blessed be Jesus Christ, true God and true man.
Blessed be the Name of Jesus.
Blessed be his most Sacred Heart.
Blessed be his most Precious Blood.
Blessed be Jesus in the most holy Sacrament of the altar.
Blessed be the Holy Spirit, the Paraclete.
Blessed be the great Mother of God, Mary most holy.
Blessed be her holy and Immaculate Conception.

Blessed be her glorious Assumption.
Blessed be the name of Mary, Virgin and Mother.
Blessed be Saint Joseph, her most chaste Spouse.
Blessed be God in his Angels and in his Saints.

Adoro Te Devote

I adore you devoutly, Godhead unseen,
who truly lies hidden under these sacramental forms.
My soul surrenders itself to you without reserve,
for in contemplating you it is completely overwhelmed.

Sight, touch, and taste are no guide in finding you,
and only hearing is a sure guide for our faith.
I believe everything that the Son of God has said,
and nothing can be truer than this Word of the truth.

Only the Godhead was hidden on
the Cross,
but here the humanity is hidden as well.
Yet I believe and acknowledge them both
and make the same request as did the
repentant thief.

I do not see the marks of the wounds, as
Thomas did,
and yet I, too, own you as "My God."
Grant that I believe in you more
and more,
that I put my hope in you and that I
love you.

Living Bread, that ever recalls
the Lord's death and gives life to
his servants,
grant to my soul to live by you
and always to taste your sweetness.

Lord Jesus, loving Pelican of heaven,*
cleanse me, a sinner, with your Blood;
for a single drop can save
the whole world from all its sin.

Jesus, as I look on your veiled presence,
I pray that what I long for so ardently
may come about,
and that I may see your face unveiled
and be happy in the vision of your glory.

[Attributed to St. Thomas Aquinas
(1225-1274)]

* The pelican is an ancient symbol of the eucharistic Lord. It was believed that in times of want, a mother pelican would feed her children with her own blood.

Ave Verum Corpus

Hail, true Body, born of the Virgin Mary,
who truly suffered, was sacrificed on the
Cross for us,
from whose pierced side flowed water
and blood.
Be from us a foretaste of heaven in the
final trial of death,
O sweet Jesus, O loving Jesus, O Jesus
Son of Mary.

[from *Holy Communion and Worship of the Eucharist Outside Mass* (2024)]

Corpus Christi Sequence (*Lauda Sion*)

Laud, O Zion, your salvation,
Laud with hymns of exultation,
    Christ, your king and shepherd true:

Bring him all the praise you know,
He is more than you bestow.
    Never can you reach his due.

Special theme for glad thanksgiving
Is the quick'ning and the living
    Bread today before you set:

From his hands of old partaken,
As we know, by faith unshaken,
    Where the Twelve at supper met.

Full and clear ring out your chanting,
Joy nor sweetest grace be wanting,
    From your heart let praises burst:

For today the feast is holden,
When the institution olden
    Of that supper was rehearsed.

Here the new law's new oblation,
By the new king's revelation,
  Ends the form of ancient rite:

Now the new the old effaces,
Truth away the shadow chases,
  Light dispels the gloom of night.

What he did at supper seated,
Christ ordained to be repeated,
  His memorial ne'er to cease:

And his rule for guidance taking,
Bread and wine we hallow, making
  Thus our sacrifice of peace.

This the truth each Christian learns,
Bread into his flesh he turns,
  To his precious blood the wine:

Sight has fail'd, nor thought conceives,
But a dauntless faith believes,
  Resting on a pow'r divine.

Here beneath these signs are hidden
Priceless things to sense forbidden;
  Sign, not things are all we see:

Blood is poured and flesh is broken,
Yet in either wondrous token
Christ entire we know to be.

Whoso of this food partakes,
Does not rend the Lord nor breaks;
Christ is whole to all that tastes:

Thousands are, as one, receivers,
One, as thousands of believers,
Eats of him who cannot waste.

Bad and good the feast are sharing,
Of what divers dooms preparing,
Endless death, or endless life.

Life to these, to those damnation,
See how like participation
Is with unlike issues rife.

When the sacrament is broken,
Doubt not, but believe 'tis spoken,
That each sever'd outward token
doth the very whole contain.

Nought the precious gift divides,
Breaking but the sign betides
Jesus still the same abides,
still unbroken does remain.

Lo! the angel's food is given
To the pilgrim who has striven;
  See the children's bread from heaven,
   which on dogs may not be spent.

Truth the ancient types fulfilling,
Isaac bound, a victim willing,
  Paschal lamb, its lifeblood spilling,
  manna to the fathers sent.

Very bread, good shepherd, tend us,
Jesu, of your love befriend us,
  You refresh us, you defend us,
  Your eternal goodness send us
In the land of life to see.

You who all things can and know,
Who on earth such food bestow,
  Grant us with your saints, though
   lowest,
  Where the heav'nly feast you show,
Fellow heirs and guests to be. Amen.
   Alleluia.

[*Sequence composed by St. Thomas Aquinas.*]

Ubi Caritas

The love of Christ has gathered us
 into one.
Let us rejoice and take delight in it.
Let us fear and love the living God,
And let us love one another with a
 sincere heart.

Where charity is true, there is God.
Therefore when we are gathered together
 as one
Let us take care lest we be divided
 in mind.
Let malicious strife be ended, let
 quarrels cease,
And may Christ God be in our midst.

Where charity is true, there is God.
Together also with the blessed
May we see your face in glory,
 Christ God,
Joy immense and good,
For endless ages of ages. Amen.

LITANIES

Litany of the Holy Name of Jesus

Lord, have mercy	Lord, have mercy
Christ, have mercy	Christ, have mercy
Lord, have mercy	Lord, have mercy
God our Father in heaven	have mercy on us
God the Son, Redeemer of the world	have mercy on us
God the Holy Spirit	have mercy on us
Holy Trinity, one God	have mercy on us
Jesus, Son of the living God	have mercy on us
Jesus, splendor of the Father	have mercy on us
Jesus, brightness of everlasting light	have mercy on us
Jesus, king of glory	have mercy on us

Jesus, dawn of justice — have mercy on us

Jesus, Son of the Virgin Mary — have mercy on us

Jesus, worthy of our love — have mercy on us

Jesus, worthy of our wonder — have mercy on us

Jesus, mighty God — have mercy on us

Jesus, father of the world to come — have mercy on us

Jesus, prince of peace — have mercy on us

Jesus, all-powerful — have mercy on us

Jesus, pattern of patience — have mercy on us

Jesus, model of obedience — have mercy on us

Jesus, gentle and humble of heart — have mercy on us

Jesus, lover of chastity — have mercy on us

Jesus, lover of us all — have mercy on us

Jesus, God of peace — have mercy on us

Jesus, author of life	have mercy on us
Jesus, model of goodness	have mercy on us
Jesus, seeker of souls	have mercy on us
Jesus, our God	have mercy on us
Jesus, our refuge	have mercy on us
Jesus, father of the poor	have mercy on us
Jesus, treasure of the faithful	have mercy on us
Jesus, Good Shepherd	have mercy on us
Jesus, the true light	have mercy on us
Jesus, eternal wisdom	have mercy on us
Jesus, infinite goodness	have mercy on us
Jesus, our way and our life	have mercy on us
Jesus, joy of angels	have mercy on us
Jesus, king of patriarchs	have mercy on us
Jesus, teacher of apostles	have mercy on us

Jesus, master of evangelists — have mercy on us

Jesus, courage of martyrs — have mercy on us

Jesus, light of confessors — have mercy on us

Jesus, purity of virgins — have mercy on us

Jesus, crown of all saints — have mercy on us

Lord, be merciful Jesus, — save your people

From all evil Jesus, — save your people

From every sin Jesus, — save your people

From the snares of the devil — Jesus, save your people

From your anger — Jesus, save your people

From the spirit of infidelity — Jesus, save your people

From everlasting death — Jesus, save your people

From neglect of your Holy Spirit — Jesus, save your people

By the mystery of your incarnation	Jesus, save your people
By your birth	Jesus, save your people
By your childhood	Jesus, save your people
By your hidden life	Jesus, save your people
By your public ministry	Jesus, save your people
By your agony and crucifixion	Jesus, save your people
By your abandonment	Jesus, save your people
By your grief and sorrow	Jesus, save your people
By your death and burial	Jesus, save your people
By your rising to new life	Jesus, save your people
By your return in glory to the Father	Jesus, save your people

By your gift of the holy Eucharist	Jesus, save your people
By your joy and glory	Jesus, save your people
Christ, hear us	Christ, hear us
Lord Jesus, hear our prayer	Lord Jesus, hear our prayer
Lamb of God, you take away the sins of the world	have mercy on us
Lamb of God, you take away the sins of the world	have mercy on us
Lamb of God, you take away the sins of the world	have mercy on us

Let us pray.
As we venerate the most holy Name of Jesus, mercifully grant us, Lord, that, savoring its sweetness in this life, we may be filled with everlasting joy in our heavenly homeland. Through Christ our Lord. Amen.

Litany of the Sacred Heart of Jesus

Lord, have mercy	Lord, have mercy
Christ, have mercy	Christ, have mercy
Lord, have mercy	Lord, have mercy
God our Father in heaven	have mercy on us
God the Son, Redeemer of the world	have mercy on us
God the Holy Spirit	have mercy on us
Holy Trinity, one God	have mercy on us
Heart of Jesus, Son of the eternal Father	have mercy on us
Heart of Jesus, formed by the Holy Spirit in the womb of the Virgin Mother	have mercy on us
Heart of Jesus, one with the eternal Word	have mercy on us

Heart of Jesus, infinite
in majesty — have mercy on us

Heart of Jesus, holy
temple of God — have mercy on us

Heart of Jesus,
tabernacle of
the Most High — have mercy on us

Heart of Jesus,
house of God and
gate of heaven — have mercy on us

Heart of Jesus, aflame
with love for us — have mercy on us

Heart of Jesus,
source of
justice and love — have mercy on us

Heart of Jesus,
full of goodness
and love — have mercy on us

Heart of Jesus,
wellspring of
all virtue — have mercy on us

Heart of Jesus,
worthy of all praise — have mercy on us

Heart of Jesus,
king and center
of all hearts — have mercy on us

Heart of Jesus,
treasurehouse
of wisdom
and knowledge — have mercy on us

Heart of Jesus, in
whom there dwells
the fullness of God — have mercy on us

Heart of Jesus, in
whom the Father
is well pleased — have mercy on us

Heart of Jesus, from
whose fullness we
have all received — have mercy on us

Heart of Jesus, desire
of the eternal hills — have mercy on us

Heart of Jesus, patient
and full of mercy — have mercy on us

Heart of Jesus,
generous to all
who turn to you — have mercy on us

Heart of Jesus,
fountain of life
and holiness — have mercy on us

Heart of Jesus,
atonement for
our sins — have mercy on us

Heart of Jesus,
overwhelmed
with insults — have mercy on us

Heart of Jesus, broken
for our sins — have mercy on us

Heart of Jesus,
obedient even
to death — have mercy on us

Heart of Jesus,
pierced by a lance — have mercy on us

Heart of Jesus, source
of all consolation — have mercy on us

Heart of Jesus, our life
and resurrection — have mercy on us

Heart of Jesus,
our peace and
reconciliation — have mercy on us

Heart of Jesus,
victim of our sins — have mercy on us

Heart of Jesus,
salvation of all
who trust in you — have mercy on us

Heart of Jesus, hope
of all who die in you — have mercy on us

Heart of Jesus, delight
of all the saints — have mercy on us

Lamb of God,
you take away the
sins of the world — have mercy on us

Lamb of God,
you take away the
sins of the world — have mercy on us

Lamb of God,
you take away the
sins of the world — have mercy on us

Jesus, gentle and
humble of heart. — Touch our hearts
and make them
like your own.

Let us pray.
Grant, we pray, almighty God, that we, who glory in the Heart of your beloved Son and

recall the wonders of his love for us, may be made worthy to receive an overflowing measure of grace from that fount of heavenly gifts. Though Christ our Lord. Amen.

Litany of the Most Precious Blood

Lord, have mercy	Lord, have mercy
Christ, have mercy	Christ, have mercy
Lord, have mercy	Lord, have mercy
God our Father in heaven	have mercy on us
God the Son, Redeemer of the world	have mercy on us
God the Holy Spirit	have mercy on us
Holy Trinity, one God	have mercy on us
Blood of Christ, only Son of the Father	save us
Blood of Christ, Incarnate Word	save us

Blood of Christ, of the
new and eternal covenant save us

Blood of Christ,
that spilled to the ground save us

Blood of Christ, that
flowed at the scourging save us

Blood of Christ, dripping
from the thorns save us

Blood of Christ,
shed on the Cross save us

Blood of Christ, the
price of our redemption save us

Blood of Christ,
our only claim to pardon save us

Blood of Christ,
our blessing cup save us

Blood of Christ,
in which we are washed save us

Blood of Christ,
torrent of mercy save us

Blood of Christ,
that overcomes evil save us

Blood of Christ,
strength of the martyrs save us

Blood of Christ,
endurance of the saints — save us

Blood of Christ, that
makes the barren fruitful — save us

Blood of Christ, protection
of the threatened — save us

Blood of Christ,
comfort of the weary — save us

Blood of Christ,
solace of the mourner — save us

Blood of Christ,
hope of the repentant — save us

Blood of Christ,
consolation of the dying — save us

Blood of Christ, our
peace and refreshment — save us

Blood of Christ,
our pledge of life — save us

Blood of Christ, by
which we pass to glory — save us

Blood of Christ,
most worthy of honor — save us

Lamb of God,
you take away the sins of the world — have mercy on us

Lamb of God,
you take away the sins of the world — have mercy on us

Lamb of God,
you take away the sins of the world — have mercy on us

Lord, you redeemed us by your Blood. — You have made us a kingdom to serve our God.

Let us pray.
O God, who by the Precious Blood of your Only Begotten Son have redeemed the whole world, preserve in us the work of your mercy, so that, ever honoring the mystery of our salvation, we may merit to obtain its fruits. Though Christ our Lord. Amen.

Litany of the Holy Eucharist

Lord, have mercy	Lord, have mercy
Christ, have mercy	Christ, have mercy
Lord, have mercy	Lord, have mercy
Jesus, the Most High	have mercy on us
Jesus, the holy One	have mercy on us
Jesus, Word of God	have mercy on us
Jesus, only Son of the Father	have mercy on us
Jesus, Son of Mary	have mercy on us
Jesus, crucified for us	have mercy on us
Jesus, risen from the dead	have mercy on us
Jesus, reigning in glory	have mercy on us
Jesus, coming in glory	have mercy on us
Jesus, our Lord	have mercy on us
Jesus, our hope	have mercy on us
Jesus, our peace	have mercy on us
Jesus, our Savior	have mercy on us

Jesus, our salvation	have mercy on us
Jesus, our resurrection	have mercy on us
Jesus, Judge of all	have mercy on us
Jesus, Lord of the Church	have mercy on us
Jesus, Lord of creation	have mercy on us
Jesus, Lover of all	have mercy on us
Jesus, life of the world	have mercy on us
Jesus, freedom for the imprisoned	have mercy on us
Jesus, joy of the sorrowing	have mercy on us
Jesus, giver of the spirit	have mercy on us
Jesus, giver of good gifts	have mercy on us
Jesus, source of new life	have mercy on us
Jesus, Lord of life	have mercy on us
Jesus, eternal high priest	have mercy on us
Jesus, priest and victim	have mercy on us
Jesus, true Shepherd	have mercy on us
Jesus, true light	have mercy on us

Jesus, bread of heaven have mercy on us

Jesus, bread of life have mercy on us

Jesus, bread of thanksgiving have mercy on us

Jesus, life-giving bread have mercy on us

Jesus, holy manna have mercy on us

Jesus, new covenant have mercy on us

Jesus, food for everlasting life have mercy on us

Jesus, food for our journey have mercy on us

Jesus, holy banquet have mercy on us

Jesus, true Sacrifice have mercy on us

Jesus, perfect Sacrifice have mercy on us

Jesus, eternal Sacrifice have mercy on us

Jesus, divine Victim have mercy on us

Jesus, Mediator of the new covenant have mercy on us

Jesus, mystery of the altar have mercy on us

Jesus, mystery of faith have mercy on us

Jesus, medicine of immortality — have mercy on us

Jesus, pledge of eternal glory — have mercy on us

Jesus, Lamb of God, you take away the sins of the world — have mercy on us

Jesus, Bearer of our sins, you take away the sins of the world — have mercy on us

Jesus, Redeemer of the world, you take away the sins of the world — have mercy on us

Christ, hear us — Christ, hear us

Christ, graciously hear us — Christ, graciously hear us

Lord Jesus, hear our prayer — Lord Jesus, hear our prayer

EXCERPTS FROM PAPAL DOCUMENTS

Venerable Pius XII, *Mystici Corporis Christi* (*On the Mystical Body of Christ*)

82. By means of the Eucharistic Sacrifice Christ our Lord willed to give the faithful a striking manifestation of our union among ourselves and with our divine Head, wonderful as it is and beyond all praise. For in this Sacrifice the sacred minister acts as the viceregent not only of our Savior but of the whole Mystical Body and of each one of the faithful. In this act of Sacrifice through the hands of the priest, by whose word alone the Immaculate Lamb is present on the altar, the faithful themselves, united with him in prayer and desire, offer to the Eternal Father a most acceptable victim of praise and propitiation for the needs of the whole Church.

And as the Divine Redeemer, when dying on the Cross, offered Himself to the Eternal Father as Head of the whole human race, so "in this clean oblation" (163) He offers to the heavenly Father not only Himself as Head of the Church, but in Himself His mystical members also, since He holds them all, even those who are weak and ailing, in His most loving Heart.

83. The Sacrament of the Eucharist is itself a striking and wonderful figure of the unity of the Church, if we consider how in the bread to be consecrated many grains go to form one whole, (164) and that in it the very Author of supernatural grace is given to us, so that through Him we may receive the spirit of charity in which we are bidden to live now no longer our own life but the life of Christ, and to love the Redeemer Himself in all the members of His social Body.

163. *Mal.*, I, 11.
164. Cf. *Didache*, IX, 4.

St. John XXIII, *Sacerdotii Nostri Primordia* (*On St. John Vianney*)

St. John Vianney's Devotion to the Eucharist

45. The devotion to prayer of St. John M. Vianney, who was to spend almost the whole of the last thirty years of his life in Church caring for the crowds of penitents who flocked to him, had one special characteristic—it was specially directed toward the Eucharist.

46. It is almost unbelievable how ardent his devotion to Christ hidden beneath the veils of the Eucharist really was. "He is the one"—he said—"Who has loved us so much; why shouldn't we love Him in return?" (59) He was devoted to the adorable Sacrament of the altar with a burning charity and his soul was drawn to the sacred Tabernacle by a heavenly force that could not be resisted.

47. This is how he taught his faithful to pray: "You do not need many words when you pray. We believe on faith that

the good and gracious God is there in the tabernacle; we open our souls to Him; and feel happy that He allows us to come before Him; this is the best way to pray." (60) He did everything that there was to be done to stir up the reverence and love of the faithful for Christ hidden in the Sacrament of the Eucharist and to bring them to share in the riches of the divine Synaxis; the example of his devotion was ever before them. "To be convinced of this—witnesses tell us—all that was necessary was to see him carrying out the sacred ceremonies or simply to see him genuflect when he passed the tabernacle." (61)

Benefits from Eucharistic Prayer

48. As Our predecessor of immortal memory, Pius XII, has said—"The wonderful example of St. John Mary Vianney retains all of its force for our times." (62) For the lengthy prayer of a priest before the adorable Sacrament of the Altar has a dignity and an effectiveness that cannot be found elsewhere nor be replaced. And so when the priest adores Christ Our Lord and gives thanks to Him, or offers satisfaction

for his own sins and those of others, or finally when he prays constantly that God keep special watch over the causes committed to his care, he is inflamed with a more ardent love for the Divine Redeemer to whom he has sworn allegiance and for those to whom he is devoting his pastoral care. And a devotion to the Eucharist that is ardent, constant and that carries over into works also has the effect of nourishing and fostering the inner perfection of his soul and assuring him, as he carries out his apostolic duties, of an abundance of the supernatural powers that the strongest workers for Christ must have.

59 Cf. *Archiv. Secret. Vat.*, v. 227, p. 1103.
60 Cf. *ibid.*, v. 227, p. 45.
61 Cf. *ibid.*, v. 227, p. 459.
62 Cf. Message of June 25, 1956: AAS 48 (1956) 579.

St. Paul VI, *Marialis Cultus (On Devotion to the Bl. Virgin Mary)*

20. Mary is, finally, the Virgin presenting offerings. In the episode of the Presentation of Jesus in the Temple (cf. Lk 2:22-35), the Church, guided by the

Spirit, has detected, over and above the fulfillment of the laws regarding the offering of the firstborn (cf. Ex 13:11-16) and the purification of the mother (cf. Lv 12:6-8), a mystery of salvation related to the history of salvation. That is, she has noted the continuity of the fundamental offering that the Incarnate Word made to the Father when He entered the world (cf. Heb 15:5-7). The Church has seen the universal nature of salvation proclaimed, for Simeon, greeting in the Child the light to enlighten the peoples and the glory of the people Israel (cf. Lk 2:32), recognized in Him the Messiah, the Savior of all. The Church has understood the prophetic reference to the Passion of Christ: the fact that Simeon's words, which linked in one prophecy the Son as "the sign of contradiction" (Lk. 2:34) and the Mother, whose soul would be pierced by a sword (cf. Lk 2:35), came true on Calvary. A mystery of salvation, therefore, that in its various aspects orients the episode of the Presentation in the Temple to the salvific event of the cross. But the Church herself, in particular from the Middle Ages onwards, has detected in the heart of the Virgin taking her Son to Jerusalem to present Him to the Lord (cf. Lk 2:22) a desire to make an offering, a desire that exceeds the ordinary meaning of the rite. A witness to this intuition is found in the loving prayer of Saint Bernard "Offer your Son, holy Virgin, and present to the Lord the blessed fruit of your womb. Offer for the reconciliation of us all the holy Victim which is pleasing to God." (56)

This union of the Mother and the Son in the work of redemption (57) reaches its climax on Calvary, where Christ "offered himself as the perfect sacrifice to God" (Heb 9:14) and where Mary stood by the cross (cf. Jn 19:25), "suffering grievously with her only-begotten Son. There she united herself with a maternal heart to His sacrifice, and lovingly consented to the immolation of this victim which she herself had brought forth" (58) and also was offering to the eternal Father." (59) To perpetuate down the centuries the Sacrifice of the Cross, the divine Savior instituted the Eucharistic sacrifice, the memorial of

His death and resurrection, and entrusted it to His spouse the Church, (60) which, especially on Sundays, calls the faithful together to celebrate the Passover of the Lord until He comes again. (61) This the Church does in union with the saints in heaven and in particular with the Blessed Virgin, (62) whose burning charity and unshakable faith she imitates.

56 *In Purificatione*, B. Mariae, Sermo III, 2: PL 183, 370; Sancti Bernardi Opera, ed J. Leclercq-H. Rochais, vol IV, Rome 1966. p. 342.
57 Cf. II Vatican Council Dogmatic Constitution on the Church, *Lumen Gentium* 57: AAS 57 (1965), p. 61.
58 Ibid, 58: AAS 57 (1965), p. 61.
59 Cf. Pius XII Encyclical Letter *Mystici Corporis*: AAS 35 (1943), P. 247.
60 Cf. II Vatican Council, Constitution on the Sacred Liturgy, *Sacrosanctum Concilium*, 47: AAS 56 (1964), pp. 113.
61 Ibid. 102, 106: AAS 56 (1964), pp. 125, 126.

St. Paul VI, *Mysterium Fidei* (*On the Holy Eucharist*)

67. No one can fail to see that the divine Eucharist bestows an incomparable dignity upon the Christian people. For it is not just while the Sacrifice is being offered and

the Sacrament is being confected, but also after the Sacrifice has been offered and the Sacrament confected—while the Eucharist is reserved in churches or oratories—that Christ is truly Emmanuel, which means "God with us." For He is in the midst of us day and night; He dwells in us with the fullness of grace and of truth. (68) He raises the level of morals, fosters virtue, comforts the sorrowful, strengthens the weak and stirs up all those who draw near to Him to imitate Him, so that they may learn from his example to be meek and humble of heart, and to seek not their own interests but those of God. Anyone who has a special devotion to the sacred Eucharist and who tries to repay Christ's infinite love for us with an eager and unselfish love of his own, will experience and fully understand—and this will bring great delight and benefit to his soul—just how precious is a life hidden with Christ in God (69) and just how worthwhile it is to carry on a conversation with Christ, for there is nothing more consoling here on earth, nothing more efficacious for progress along the paths of holiness. …

69. Hence it is that devotion to the divine Eucharist exerts a great influence upon the soul in the direction of fostering a "social" love, (71) in which we put the common good ahead of private good, take up the cause of the community, the parish, the universal Church, and extend our charity to the whole world because we know that there are members of Christ everywhere. . . .

75. May the most blessed Virgin Mary, from whom Christ the Lord took the flesh that "is contained, offered, received" (81) in this Sacrament under the appearances of bread and wine, and may all the saints of God and especially those who were more inflamed with ardent devotion toward the divine Eucharist, intercede with the Father of mercies so that this common belief in the Eucharist and devotion to it may give rise among all Christians to a perfect unity of communion that will continue to flourish. Lingering in Our mind are the words of the holy martyr Ignatius warning the Philadelphians against the evil of divisions and schisms, the remedy for which is to be found in the Eucharist. "Strive then," he says, "to make use of one single

thanksgiving. For there is only one flesh of Our Lord Jesus Christ, and only one chalice unto the union of His blood, only one altar, only one bishop …" (82)

68 Cf. *Jn* 1:14.
69 Cf. *Col* 3:3.

71 Cf. St. Augustine, *On the literal interpretation of Genesis* XI, 15.20; PL 34.437.

81 C.I.C., canon 801.
82 *Epistle to the Philadelphians* 4; PG 5.700.

St. John Paul II, *Ecclesia de Eucharistia (On the Eucharist)*

25. … It is pleasant to spend time with him, to lie close to his breast like the Beloved Disciple (cf. Jn 13:25) and to feel the infinite love present in his heart. If in our time Christians must be distinguished above all by the "art of prayer", (48) how can we not feel a renewed need to spend time in spiritual converse, in silent adoration, in heartfelt love before Christ present in the Most Holy Sacrament? How often, dear brother and sisters, have I experienced this, and drawn from it strength, consolation and support!

This practice, repeatedly praised and recommended by the Magisterium, (49) is supported by the example of many saints. Particularly outstanding in this regard was Saint Alphonsus Liguori, who wrote: "Of all devotions, that of adoring Jesus in the Blessed Sacrament is the greatest after the sacraments, the one dearest to God and the one most helpful to us." (50) The Eucharist is a priceless treasure: by not only celebrating it but also by praying before it outside of Mass we are enabled to make contact with the very wellspring of grace. ...

61. The mystery of the Eucharist—sacrifice, presence, banquet—*does not allow for reduction or exploitation*; it must be experienced and lived in its integrity, both in its celebration and in the intimate converse with Jesus which takes place after receiving communion or in a prayerful moment of Eucharistic adoration apart from Mass. These are times when the Church is firmly built up and it becomes clear what she truly is: one, holy, catholic and apostolic; the people, temple and family of God; the body and bride of Christ, enlivened by

the Holy Spirit; the universal sacrament of salvation and a hierarchically structured communion.

48 John Paul II, Apostolic Letter *Novo Millennio Ineunte* (6 January 2001), 32: AAS 93 (2001), 288.

49 "In the course of the day the faithful should not omit visiting the Blessed Sacrament, which in accordance with liturgical law must be reserved in churches with great reverence in a prominent place. Such visits are a sign of gratitude, an expression of love and an acknowledgment of the Lord's presence": Paul VI, Encyclical Letter *Mysterium Fidei* (3 September 1965): AAS 57 (1965), 771.

50 *Visite al SS. Sacramento e a Maria Santissima*, Introduction: *Opere Ascetiche*, Avellino, 2000, 295.

St. John Paul II, *Dominicae Cenae (On the Mystery and Worship of the Eucharist)*

Worship of the Eucharistic Mystery

3. This worship is directed towards God the Father through Jesus Christ in the Holy Spirit. In the first place towards the Father, who, as St. John's Gospel says, "loved the world so much that he gave his only Son, so that everyone who believes in him may not be lost but may have eternal life." (9)

It is also directed, in the Holy Spirit, to the incarnate Son, in the economy of salvation, especially at that moment of supreme dedication and total abandonment of Himself to which the words uttered in the Upper Room refer: "This is my body given up for you. ... This is the cup of my blood shed for you. ..." (10) The liturgical acclamation: "We proclaim your death, Lord Jesus" takes us back precisely to that moment; and with the proclamation of His resurrection we embrace in the same act of veneration Christ risen and glorified "at the right hand of the Father," as also the expectation of His "coming in glory." Yet it is the voluntary emptying of Himself, accepted by the Father and glorified with the resurrection, which, sacramentally celebrated together with the resurrection brings us to adore the Redeemer who "became obedient unto death, even death on a cross." (11)

And this adoration of ours contains yet another special characteristic. It is compenetrated by the greatness of that human death, in which the world, that is to say each one of us, has been loved "to the end." (12) Thus it is also a response that tries to repay that love immolated even to the death on the cross: it is our "Eucharist," that is to say our giving Him thanks, our praise of Him for having redeemed us by His death and made us sharers in immortal life through His resurrection.

This worship, given therefore to the Trinity of the Father and of the Son and of the Holy Spirit, above all accompanies and permeates the celebration of the Eucharistic Liturgy. But it must fill our churches also outside the timetable of Masses. Indeed, since the Eucharistic Mystery was instituted out of love, and makes Christ sacramentally present, it is worthy of thanksgiving and worship. And this worship must be prominent in all our encounters with the Blessed Sacrament, both when we visit our churches and when the sacred species are taken to the sick and administered to them. ...

5. ... Eucharistic worship constitutes the soul of all Christian life. In fact, Christian

life is expressed in the fulfilling of the greatest commandment, that is to say, in the love of God and neighbor, and this love finds its source in the blessed Sacrament, which is commonly called the sacrament of love.

The Eucharist signifies this charity, and therefore recalls it, makes it present and at the same time brings it about. Every time that we consciously share in it, there opens in our souls a real dimension of that unfathomable love that includes everything that God has done and continues to do for us human beings, as Christ says: "My Father goes on working, and so do I." (21) Together with this unfathomable and free gift, which is charity revealed in its fullest degree in the saving sacrifice of the Son of God, the sacrifice of which the Eucharist is the indelible sign, there also springs up within us a lively response of love. We not only know love; we ourselves begin to love. We enter, so to speak, upon the path of love and along this path make progress. Thanks to the Eucharist, the love that springs up within us from the

Eucharist develops in us, becomes deeper and grows stronger.

Eucharistic worship is therefore precisely the expression of that love which is the authentic and deepest characteristic of the Christian vocation. This worship springs from the love and serves the love to which we are all called in Jesus Christ. (22) A living fruit of this worship is the perfecting of the image of God that we bear within us, an image that corresponds to the one that Christ has revealed in us. As we thus become adorers of the Father "in spirit and truth," (23) we mature in an ever fuller union with Christ, we are ever more united to Him, and—if one may use the expression—we are ever more in harmony with Him.

The doctrine of the Eucharist, sign of unity and bond of charity, taught by St. Paul, (24) has been in subsequent times deepened by the writings of very many saints who are living examples for us of Eucharistic worship. We must always have this reality before our eyes, and at the same time we must continually try to bring it about that our own generation too may add new examples to those marvelous examples of the past, new examples no less living and eloquent, that will reflect the age to which we belong.

9 Jn 3:16. It is interesting to note how these words are taken up by the liturgy of St. John Chrysostom immediately before the words of consecration and introduce the latter: cf. *La divina Liturgia del nostro Padre Giovanni Crisostomo*, Roma-Grottaferrata 1967, pp. 104f.

10. Cf. Mt 26:26-28; Mk 14:22-25; Lk. 22:18-20; 1 Cor 11:23-5; cf. also the Eucharistic Prayers.

11. Phil. 2:8.

12. Jn. 13:1.

21. Jn. 5:17.

22. Cf. Prayer after communion of the Mass for the Twenty-Second Sunday in Ordinary Time: "Lord, you renew us at your table with the bread of life. May this food strengthen us in love and help us to serve you in each other": *Missale Romanum*, ed. cit., p. 361.

23. Jn 4:23.

24. Cf. 1 Cor 10:17; commented upon by St. Augustine: In *Evangelium Ioannis* tract. 31, 13; PL 35, 1613; also commented upon by the Ecumenical Council of Trent, Session XIII, can. 8; *Conciliorum Oecumenicorum Decreta*, ed. 3, Bologna 1973, p. 697, 7; cf. Second Vatican Ecumenical Council, Dogmatic Constitution on the Church, Lumen gentium, 7: AAS 57 (1965), p. 9.

Pope Benedict XVI, *Sacramentum Caritatis* (*The Sacrament of Charity*)

66. … In the Eucharist, the Son of God comes to meet us and desires to become one with us; eucharistic adoration is simply the natural consequence of the eucharistic celebration, which is itself the Church's supreme act of adoration. (192) Receiving the Eucharist means adoring him whom we receive. Only in this way do we become one with him, and are given, as it were, a foretaste of the beauty of the heavenly liturgy. The act of adoration outside Mass prolongs and intensifies all that takes place during the liturgical celebration itself. Indeed, "only in adoration can a profound and genuine reception mature. And it is precisely this personal encounter with the Lord that then strengthens the social mission contained in the Eucharist, which seeks to break down not only the walls that separate the Lord and ourselves, but also and especially the walls that separate us from one another." (193) …

71. Christianity's new worship includes and transfigures every aspect of life: "Whether you eat or drink, or whatever you do, do all to the glory of God" (1 Cor 10:31). Christians, in all their actions, are called to offer true worship to God. Here the intrinsically eucharistic nature of Christian life begins to take shape. The Eucharist, since it embraces the concrete, everyday existence of the believer, makes possible, day by day, the progressive transfiguration of all those called by grace to reflect the image of the Son of God (cf. Rom 8:29 ff.). There is nothing authentically human—our thoughts and affections, our words and deeds—that does not find in the sacrament of the Eucharist the form it needs to be lived to the full. Here we can see the full human import of the radical newness brought by Christ in the Eucharist: the worship of God in our lives cannot be relegated to something private and individual, but tends by its nature to permeate every aspect of our existence. Worship pleasing to God thus becomes a new way of living our whole life, each particular moment of which is lifted up,

since it is lived as part of a relationship with Christ and as an offering to God. The glory of God is the living man (cf. 1 Cor 10:31). And the life of man is the vision of God. (203)

192 Cf. *Propositio* 6.

193 Benedict XVI, Address to the Roman Curia (Dec. 22, 2005): AAS 98 (2006), 45.

203 Cf. St. Irenaeus, *Adv. Haer.*, IV, 20, 7: PG 7, 1037.

Pope Benedict, *Meditation During the Eucharistic Procession in Lourdes*

September 14, 2008

The sacred host exposed to our view speaks of this infinite power of Love manifested on the glorious Cross. The sacred host speaks to us of the incredible abasement of the One who made himself poor so as to make us rich in him, the One who accepted the loss of everything so as to win us for his Father. The sacred host is the living, efficacious and real sacrament of the eternal presence of the savior of mankind to his Church.

Pope Francis, *Gaudete et Exsultate* (*Rejoice and Be Glad*)

157. Meeting Jesus in the Scriptures leads us to the Eucharist, where the written word attains its greatest efficacy, for there the living Word is truly present. In the Eucharist, the one true God receives the greatest worship the world can give him, for it is Christ himself who is offered. When we receive him in Holy Communion, we renew our covenant with him and allow him to carry out ever more fully his work of transforming our lives.

EXCERPT FROM A BISHOPS' PASTORAL STATEMENT

The Eucharist and the Hungers of the Human Family

A Pastoral Statement Issued by the National Conference of Catholic Bishops

November 20, 1975

The word, eucharist, means "thanksgiving," and the Eucharist is the supreme act of thanks in which Christ offers perfect worship to the Father and gives Himself as the perfect gift of love to those who believe in Him. …

The Eucharistic liturgy … is simultaneously "a sacrament of love, a sign of unity, a bond of charity, a paschal banquet in which Christ is consumed, the mind is filled with grace, and a pledge of future glory is given to us" (Vatican Council II,

Constitution on the Sacred Liturgy, 47). ... it is also [fitting] ... to recall that there are many persons in our nation and our world who experience profound hungers which crave to be satisfied. There is no one of us who does not hunger in some way, or in many ways: for, besides physical hunger, human beings have deep emotional, intellectual, and spiritual hungers.

Pleasure, power, or possessions may temporarily quiet the pangs of some hungers. They cannot satisfy us on the deepest levels of our personhood. Only God can do that. "You have made us for Yourself, O God, and our hearts are restless until they rest in You" (St. Augustine, *Confessions*, 1.1).

God the Father loves us so much that He sent His only Son to become one of us and redeem us. Jesus loves us so much that, even after His death, resurrection, and ascension, He remains with us. He is, after all, Emmanuel, "God with us," but now through His living, sanctifying Spirit. We now encounter him in new ways: in other human beings; in any place where people gather in His name (Mt 18:20); in the inspired words of Holy Scripture; in His Church, particularly her liturgical celebrations; in the person of His minister; and especially in the sacraments, preeminently in the sacrament of the Eucharist.

In the Eucharist, which is Jesus really present, God satisfies our deepest hungers. The Sacrifice of the Mass is Christ's supreme act of reconciliation. "Truly partaking of the body of the Lord in the breaking of the Eucharistic bread, we are taken up in communion with Him and with one another. 'Because the bread is one, we though many, are one body, all of us who partake of the one bread' (1 Cor 10:17). In this way all of us are made members of His body (cf. 1 Cor 12:27), 'but severally members of one another (Rom 12:15)" (Vatican Council II, *Dogmatic Constitution on the Church,* 7). The Eucharist is indeed the Sacrament of Unity, "by which the unity of the Church is both signified and brought about" (Vatican Council II, *Decree on Ecumenism,* 2). ...

Men and women hunger not only for food, but also for God, not only for bread in this life but for the Bread of Life itself; for Christ, really present in the Eucharist, really received in Holy Communion, leading us to the Father. The Eucharist responds to our needs and concerns—our many hungers—as human beings. ...

1. **Hunger for God.** If we lack God, it matters little what else we have. Estranged from God, we are estranged from our own destiny and fulfillment. Human life absorbed in itself is diminished and lacking in purpose. The Eucharist is a special means given to us by Jesus for overcoming our estrangement from God. It is as Christ tells us: "The man who feeds on my flesh and drinks my blood remains in me, and I in him" (Jn 6:56).
2. **Hunger for Bread.** Many persons today are physically hungry. Certainly the solution to starvation and malnutrition requires increased production and improved distribution of food. But it also requires "a concerted act

of solidarity" by the nations and peoples of the world (Synod of Bishops, 1974, *Statement on Human Rights and Reconciliation*). Our sharing in the Eucharist inspires us to such solidarity, as well as to actions which express it; for sincere celebration of the Eucharist "must lead to various works of charity and mutual help" (Vatican Council II, *Decree on the Ministry and Life of Priests*, 6).

3. **Hunger for Freedom and Justice.** The quest for human freedom and justice is not optional for Catholics, nor is it a small part of the Church's mission. Participation in the struggle for freedom and justice is a duty for each one of us, as it is a central element of the Church's mission of redemption and liberation. In the Eucharist we find the source of our deepest commitment to the loving service of our brothers and sisters. …
4. **Hunger for the Spirit.** In considering this theme, the Eucharistic Congress will focus in a special way on religious vocations and the need

for commitment by the clergy and religious of the world. It is most appropriate that this be done in the context of the Eucharist, for it is the special role of the clergy and religious to give witness to the transcendent, God-centered nature of human life and striving, which the Eucharist supremely expresses. This is no "perishable food but … food that remains unto life eternal, food which the Son of Man will give you" (Jn 6:27).

5. **Hunger for Truth.** Jesus proclaimed that He is "the Way, the Truth, and the Life" (Jn 14:6). we see, therefore, that knowledge of truth in the act of faith means more than just an intellectual understanding of abstract concepts. It also means commitment to a Person. Our most direct and profound encounter with this Person who is Truth occurs in the sacrament of the Eucharist. Here grace strengthens both our acceptance of what faith teaches and our loving commitment to the Person who stands at the center of faith.

6. **Hunger for Understanding.** Our times experience the tragedy of estrangement between nations, races, classes, churches, and even generations. Members of the same family are sometimes strangers to each other. Children feel that they are not understood by their parents; parents feel the same way with respect to their children. The need for reconciliation is clear. How better to achieve such reconciliation than at the Table of the Lord; for "the liturgy in its turn inspires the faithful to become of one heart in love" (Vatican Council II, *Constitution on the Sacred Liturgy*, 10).
7. **Hunger for Peace.** In an era of tension and violence, the limits of human instruments for peace are all too evident. Christ is our peace, and Christ Himself in the Eucharist provides us with both our model and best hope for peace. For it is He "who made the two of us one by breaking down the barrier of hostility that kept us apart" (Eph 2:4). It is here, in the Eucharist, that "all education in the spirit of

community must originate" (Vatican Council II, *Decree on the Ministry and Life of Priests*, 6).

8. **Hunger for Jesus—The Bread of Life.** All men and women hunger for Christ, consciously or not. It is the Lord, worthily and maturely received in Holy Communion, who brings about our loving unity with one another and with Him. Without the Eucharist, our lives in all their dimensions would be lacking in something essential; in the Eucharist we find means to conquer our weakness and tendency to sin and to live according to God's will for us. "Let me solemnly assure you if you do not eat the flesh of the Son of Man and drink his blood, you have no life in you. He who feeds on my flesh and drinks my blood has life eternal, and I will raise him up on the last day" (Jn 6:53-54).

The mysterious reality of the Eucharist—"My flesh is real food and my blood real drink" (Jn 6:55)—is a puzzle to some, a scandal to others. It has always been so.

After Jesus promised the Eucharist, "many of his disciples remarked, 'This sort of talk is hard to endure! How can anyone take it seriously? ... From this time on, many of his disciples broke away and would not remain in his company any longer" (Jn 6:60-66).

But for those who believe in Jesus' teaching because they believe in Jesus Christ Himself, the Eucharist is, among all his gifts to us, the most cherished and the cause of our deepest gratitude. After some of His disciples had left Him, Jesus asked the Twelve: "Do you want to leave me too?" Simon Peter answered—for them and for us. "Lord, to whom shall we go? You have the words of eternal life. We have come to believe; we are convinced that you are God's holy one" (Jn 6:67-69). Let us pray ... to renew our faith, our hope, our love, and our gratitude for the great gift of Our Lord and Savior Jesus Christ in the sacrament of the Eucharist; and to recommit ourselves, in union with Him, to the task of responding generously to the hungers of the human family.